UPDATED EDITION

Activity Book 2

with Digital Pack

T0372626

British English

Susan Rivers

Series Editor: Lesley Koustaff

Shaftesbury Road, Cambridge CB2 8EA, United Kingdom

One Liberty Plaza, 20th Floor, New York, NY 10006, USA

477 Williamstown Road, Port Melbourne, VIC 3207, Australia

314–321, 3rd Floor, Plot 3, Splendor Forum, Jasola District Centre, New Delhi – 110025, India

103 Penang Road, #05–06/07, Visioncrest Commercial, Singapore 238467

Cambridge University Press & Assessment is a department of the University of Cambridge.

We share the University's mission to contribute to society through the pursuit of education, learning and research at the highest international levels of excellence.

www.cambridge.org
Information on this title: www.cambridge.org/9781009480635

© Cambridge University Press & Assessment 2014, 2024

This publication is in copyright. Subject to statutory exception and to the provisions of relevant collective licensing agreements, no reproduction of any part may take place without the written permission of Cambridge University Press & Assessment.

First published 2014
Updated edition 2024

20 19 18 17 16 15 14 13 12 11 10 9 8 7 6 5 4 3

Printed in Malaysia by Vivar Printing

A catalogue record for this publication is available from the British Library

ISBN 978-1-009-48063-5 Activity Book with Digital Pack Level 2
ISBN 978-1-009-48059-8 Pupil's Book with eBook Level 2
ISBN 978-1-009-79839-6 Teacher's Book with Digital Pack Level 2
ISBN 978-1-107-52796-6 Flashcards Level 2

Additional resources for this publication at www.cambridge.org/guesswhatue

Cambridge University Press & Assessment has no responsibility for the persistence or accuracy of URLs for external or third-party internet websites referred to in this publication, and does not guarantee that any content on such websites is, or will remain, accurate or appropriate. Information regarding prices, travel timetables, and other factual information given in this work is correct at the time of first printing but Cambridge University Press & Assessment does not guarantee the accuracy of such information thereafter.

Contents

Hello again!

1 **Order the letters. Look and draw lines.**

1 eLo ___Leo___   2 dvaiD _____   3 neB _____

4 iiaOvl _____   5 aTin _____

2 **Look at Activity 1 and tick ✓.**

		yes		no	
1	This is Ben.	yes	☐	no	✓
2	This is David.	yes	☐	no	☐
3	This is Leo.	yes	☐	no	☐
4	This is Olivia.	yes	☐	no	☐
5	This is Tina.	yes	☐	no	☐

3 **Listen and stick.**

1 ⬜

2 ⬜

3 ⬜

4 ⬜

5 ⬜

4 **Look, read and match.**

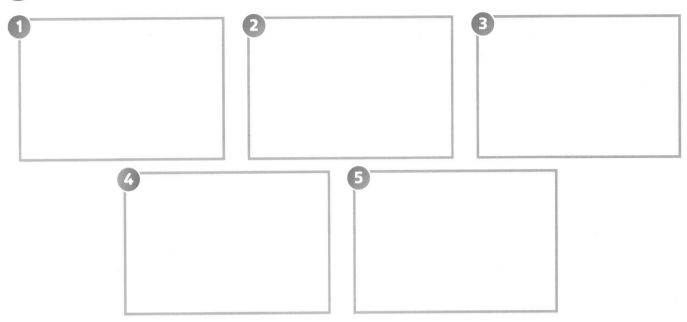

1

2

This is my ←	nine.
Her →	friend.
She's	name's Sue.

This is my	eight.
He's	name's Dan.
His	brother.

My picture dictionary → Go to page 84: Tick the words you know and trace.

Vocabulary and Grammar **5**

5 🎧 0.08 Listen and circle the name.

1

(Tom) / Don

2

Pam / Pat

3

Rick / Nick

4

Katy / Mary

6 (About Me) Draw and say. Then circle and write.

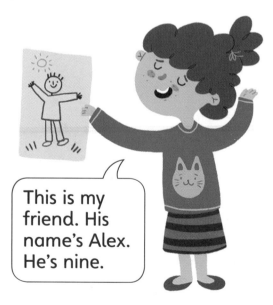

This is my friend. His name's Alex. He's nine.

This is _____ .
His / Her name's _____ .
He's / She's _____ .

7 Look, read and circle the answer.

What's this?

(It's a door.) / They're doors.

What are these?

It's a pencil. / They're pencils.

What's this?

It's a rubber. / They're rubbers.

What are these?

They're pens. / It's a pen.

8 Think Look and write

What are ___these___ ?

___They're books___ .

What's _____ ?

It's _____ .

What _____ ?

_____ .

What _____ ?

_____ .

9 🎧 0.12 **Read and number. Then listen and check.**

a

b

c

d

e

f

10 What's missing? Look and draw. Then stick.

I play with my friends.

11 Trace the letters.

The rabbit can run.
The lion is lazy.

12 Listen and circle *l* or *r*.

①

l (r)

②

l r

③

l r

④

l r

What type of **art** is it?

1 Look, read and circle the word.

1

painting / ⟨drawing⟩

2

photography / painting

3

photography / painting

4

drawing / sculpture

2 Look and copy the painting.

Evaluation

1 **Look and write the name.**

1	2	3	4	5
L e o	T _ _ _	B _ _	O _ _ _ _ _	D _ _ _ _

2 **What's your favourite part? Use your stickers.**

story   song   video

○ ○ ○

3 **Puzzle** **What's different? Circle and write.**
Then go to page 93 and write the letters.

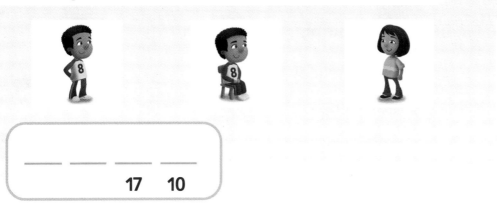

____ ____ ____
        17   10

Transport

1 Look, read and tick ✓ or cross ✗.

1 boat ✓

2 plane ☐

3 tractor ☐

4 car ☐

5 train ☐

6 motorbike ☐

2 Follow the transport words.

Start→	train	lorry	ruler	chair
	desk	bus	plane	camera
	book	painting	helicopter	table
	pencil	drawing	tractor	boat

Well done!

3 🎧1.05 🏷️ Listen and stick.

1	2	3

4	5

4 Think Look, read and write the words.

lorry boat helicopter car motorbike plane train bus

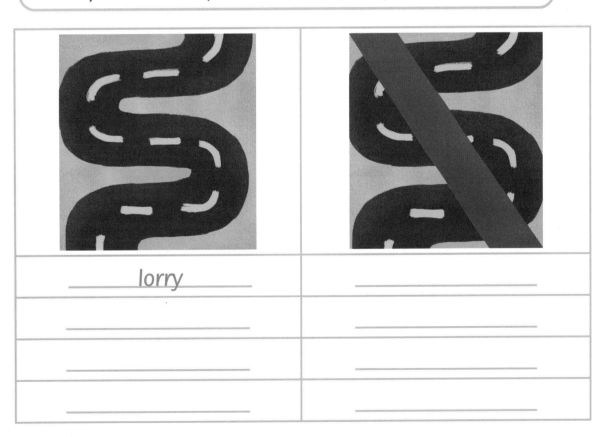

lorry	

My picture dictionary → Go to page 85: Tick the words you know and trace.

5 🎧 1.08 **Listen and tick ✓ .**

1	2	3	4
a	a	a	a
b ✓	b	b	b

6 **Look at the pictures and say.**

In picture A, he's got a car. In picture B, he's got a bus.

7 **Look, read and circle the answer.**

1

Has she got a boat?
Yes, she has. / No, she hasn't.

2

Has he got a tractor?
Yes, he has. / No, he hasn't.

3

Has he got a plane?
Yes, he has. / No, he hasn't.

4

Has she got a helicopter?
Yes, she has. / No, she hasn't.

8 **Look at the picture and answer the questions.**

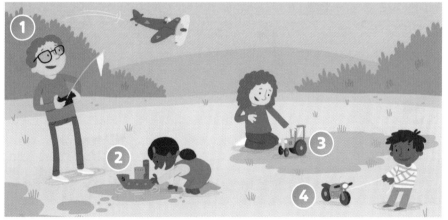

1 Has he got a train?
No, he hasn't.

2 Has she got a boat?

3 Has she got a tractor?

4 Has he got a bus?

9 **Draw and say. Then circle and write.**

This is my friend.
He's/She's got a
_____ .

10 🎧 1.12 Read and write the letter. Then listen and check.

a (Yes, of course.) **b** (It's OK.) **c** (Has Ben got a robot?)

d (Wow! The helicopter is iPal!) **e** (Thank you. This is fun!)

f (Ben's got a helicopter!)

1

f

Let's go to the park!

2

No, he hasn't. It's a helicopter.

3

Can I have a turn, please?

4

Be careful, iPal!

5

Sorry. Now let's play with my helicopter!

6

11 **What's missing? Look and draw. Then stick.**

a

b

c

I take turns. ☺

12 **Trace the letters.**

A gorilla in the garden. A hippo in a house.

13 🎧 1.15 **Listen and match the pictures with g or h.**

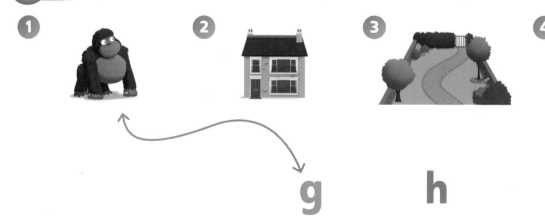

1 2 3 4

g h

Where is the transport?

1 Look, read and circle the words.

1

on land
(on water)
in the air

2

on land
on water
in the air

3

on land
on water
in the air

4

on land
on water
in the air

5

on land
on water
in the air

6

on land
on water
in the air

2 Look and draw. Say.

It's a helicopter. It's in the air.

Evaluation

1 〔Think〕 **Look, match and write the word.**

plane

2 **What's your favourite part? Use your stickers.**

story   song   video

3 〔Puzzle〕 **What's different? Circle and write. Then go to page 93 and write the letters.**

8   1

2 Pets

1 Think Order the letters and match.

1 nma _man_

2 lirg _____

3 mwnoa _____

4 yob _____

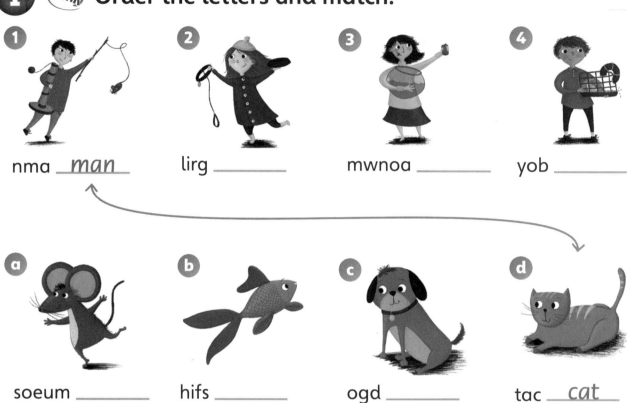

a soeum _____

b hifs _____

c ogd _____

d tac _cat_

2 What's next? Look and circle the word.

1 (girl) / boy

2 fish / frog

3 baby / woman

4 cat / dog

20 Vocabulary

3 **Listen and stick.**

1
2
3

4
5

4 **Write the words and find.**

1

men

3

2

4

c	h	i	l	d	r	e	n
n	b	j	k	l	o	p	l
b	c	m	e	n	s	a	o
c	y	m	b	c	g	h	j
v	t	m	w	o	m	e	n
m	e	e	t	y	u	k	a
a	w	b	a	b	i	e	s
q	n	e	r	t	f	n	c

My picture dictionary → Go to page 86: Tick the words you know and trace.

5 Look, write the words and match.

| ~~ugly~~ happy old beautiful sad young |

1 _ugly_ ← **a** _____

2 _____ **b** _____

3 _____ **c** _____

6 Look, read and tick ✓.

1 **2**

3 **4**

1 They're happy. ✓   They're sad. ☐

2 It's big. ☐   It's small. ☐

3 She's young. ☐   She's old. ☐

4 He's beautiful. ☐   He's ugly. ☐

7 (About Me) Draw and say. Then write.

This is my cat. It's small. It's beautiful.

This is my _____ . It's _____ . It's _____ .

8 **Listen and circle the answer.**

Yes, she is. / No, she isn't.

Yes, they are. / No, they aren't.

Yes, it is. / No, it isn't.

Yes, he is. / No, he isn't.

9 **Look at the picture and answer the questions.**

1   Is it beautiful? ___No, it isn't.___   2   Are they happy? _____

3   Is it ugly? _____   4   Are they old? _____

5   Are they young? _____   6   Are they sad? _____

cat ~~frog~~ beautiful What's you sad

1

Look! What's that?

It's a __frog__!

2

It's Aunt Sue! Hello.

Oh dear! She's _____.

3

Can we help?

Yes, please. I can't find my _____.

4

Mr Tom. He's big … and he's _____!

What's his name?

MISSING

5

_____ that?

6

Thank _____.

You're welcome!

What's missing? Look and draw. Then stick.

I am helpful. ☺

12 **Trace the letters.**

A fox with a fish.
A vulture with
vegetables.

13 (2.14) **Listen and tick ✓ v or f.**

1	v ☐ f ✓	2	v ☐ f ☐
3	v ☐ f ☐	4	v ☐ f ☐

Value   Pronunciation: v, f   **25**

What do **animals** need?

1 **Look, read and match.**

1 Animals need food.

2 Animals need water.

3 Animals need shelter.

4 Animals need sleep.

2 **Look at the picture and tick ✓ the box.**

1	A mouse needs shelter.	☐
2	A mouse needs food.	☐
3	A mouse needs water.	☐

Evaluation

1 **Read and write the answer.**

1 This pet can climb trees. It likes mice and fish. _cat_

2 This pet swims in water. It hasn't got legs. _____

3 This pet is very small. It has got four short legs and
  a long tail. _____

4 This pet likes the water. It's got long legs and can jump. _____

5 This pet has got four legs and a tail. It isn't a cat. _____

2 **What's your favourite part? Use your stickers.**

story   song   video

3 **Puzzle** **What's different? Circle and write.**
Then go to page 93 and write the letters.

____ ____ ____ ____
 2   14

Review Units 1 and 2

1 Look and write the word.

Crossword:
- 9. t
- 1. o

2 Read and circle the answer.

1 What are … ?
They're books.
   a this   b (these)

3 … babies.
   a It's   b They're

5 … she … a boat?
   a Has, got   b Got, has

2 He's … a motorbike.
   a got   b has

4 How do you … Leo? L-E-O
   a spell   b name

6 Is … beautiful? Yes, … is.
   a it, it   b they, they

3 Look, read and match.

1

How do you spell Lucy?

2

What are these?

3

Has she got a fish?

4

Are they old?

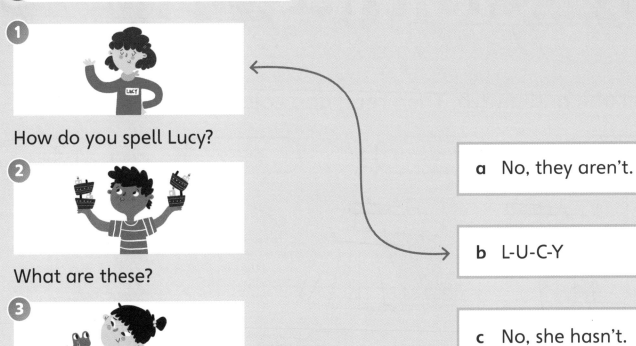

a No, they aren't.

b L-U-C-Y

c No, she hasn't.

d They're boats.

4 🎧 2.17 Listen and tick ✓.

1

2

3 Clothes

1 **Look and match. Then read and colour.**

| shoes | jacket | dress | T-shirt |

| skirt | socks | jeans | shirt | trousers |

1 Colour the shoes black.
2 Colour the trousers green.
3 Colour the jacket yellow.
4 Colour the T-shirt purple.
5 Colour the jeans blue.
6 Colour the skirt orange.
7 Colour the shirt red.
8 Colour the socks blue.
9 Colour the dress pink.

2 🎧 3.05 📝 **Listen and stick.**

1	2	3

4	5

3 Think **Look and write the words.**

socks̶ jeans T-shirt skirt
trousers shirt shoes jacket

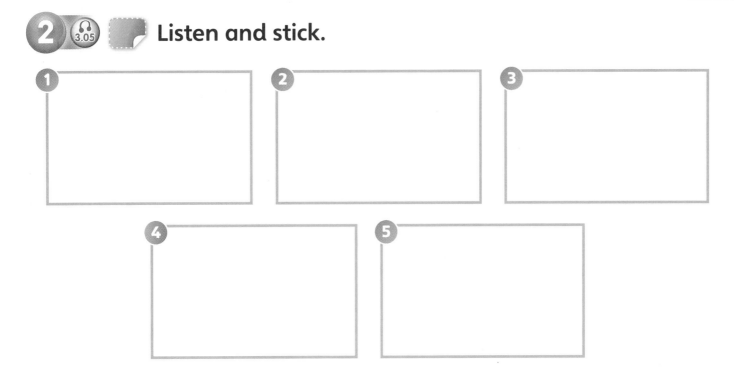

1 _____

2 _____ →

3 _____

4 _____

5 _____ →

6 _____

7 <u>socks</u> →

8 _____

My picture dictionary → Go to page 87: Tick the words you know and trace.

4 Look, read and tick ✓.

1

What are you wearing?
I'm wearing trousers and a shirt.

2

What are you wearing?
I'm wearing a dress and shoes.

3
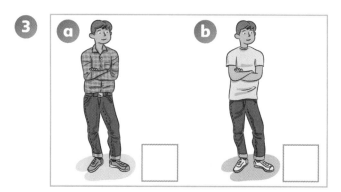

What are you wearing?
I'm wearing jeans and a T-shirt.

4

What are you wearing?
I'm wearing a skirt and a shirt.

5 Look at the pictures and write.

1   **2**   **3**   **4**

1 I'm wearing ___*a skirt*___ , ___*a T-shirt*___ and ___*shoes*___ .
2 I'm wearing _____ , _____ and _____ .
3 I'm wearing _____ , _____ and _____ .
4 I'm wearing _____ , _____ and _____ .

6 🎧 3.10 **Listen and number the pictures.**

a   b   c

7 **Look, read and circle the word.**

1

Are you wearing a (skirt) / **dress**?
No, I'm not.

2

Are you wearing a **shirt** / **T-shirt**?
Yes, I am.

3

Are you wearing **shoes** / **socks**?
No, I'm not.

4

Are you wearing **trousers** / **jeans**?
Yes, I am.

8 (About Me) **Draw. Ask and answer with a friend.**

Are you wearing a skirt?

No, I'm not.

9 Read and number. Then listen and check.

10 **Look, read and stick.**

I share things.

11 **Trace the letters.**

Jackals don't like jelly. Yaks don't like yoghurt.

12 3.15 **Listen and circle *j* or *y*.**

1   2   3   4

(j) y   j y   j y   j y

What are **clothes** made of?

1 Look and write the number.

wool ☐   silk ☐   leather ☐   cotton 1

2 Look, read and circle the word.

wool /(silk)   leather / cotton   wool / silk   cotton / leather

Evaluation

1 Write the words and find.

1

socks

2
_____

3
_____

4
_____

5
_____

```
g s k i r t f s h o e s d
f s d r e s s d v b c m q
j e a n s n a j k o a l o
a w t r o u s e r s p l l
s o c k s m c n v b w i k
```

6
_____

2 What's your favourite part? Use your stickers.

 story

 song

 video

3 **Puzzle** What's different? Circle and write.
Then go to page 93 and write the letters.

____ ____ ____ ____ ____ ____
11   12

1 Look, read and circle the word.

wardrobe / (bookcase)

lamp / mirror

TV / phone

sofa / cupboard

clock / TV

bookcase / table

2 Look, read and write.

It isn't a cupboard. It isn't a bookcase. It's a __wardrobe__ .

It isn't a mirror. It isn't a lamp. It's a _____ .

It isn't a table. It isn't a bed. It's a _____ .

It isn't a TV. It isn't a lamp. It's a _____ .

3 🎧 4.05 📄 **Listen and stick.**

1	2	3

4	5

4 (Think) **Look, match and write the words.**

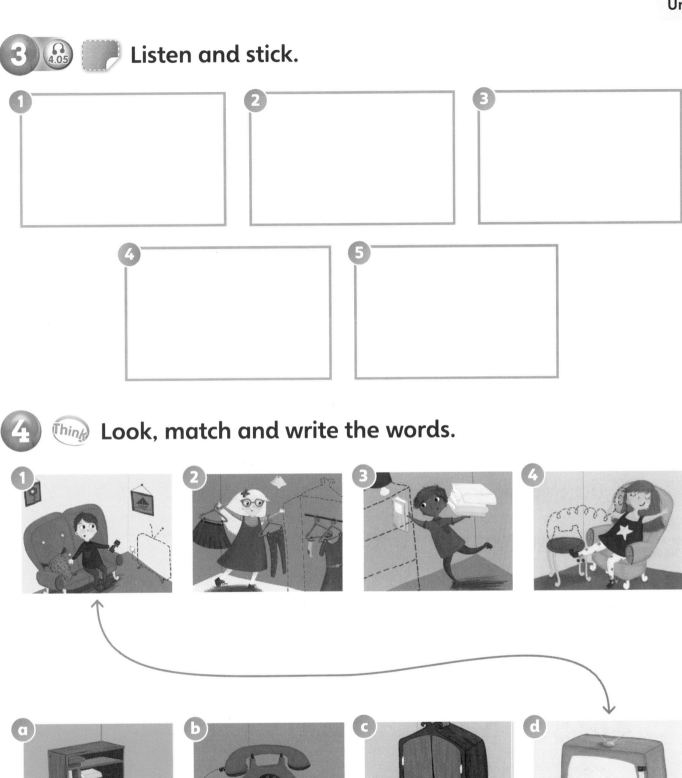

a _____

b _____

c _____

d ___TV___

 My picture dictionary ➡ Go to page 88: Tick the words you know and trace.

5 Look, read and write *yes* or *no*.

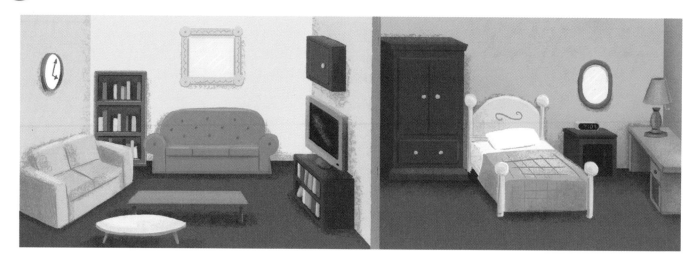

1 There are four lamps in the bedroom. *no*
2 There are two sofas in the living room. _____
3 There are two clocks in the bedroom. _____
4 There's a wardrobe in the living room. _____
5 There's a bookcase in the living room. _____
6 There's a mirror in the bedroom. _____

6 (About Me) Draw your room and say. Then write.

There's a lamp in my room.

There are two tables in my room.

There's a _____ in my room.
There are _____
_____ in my room.

7 (Think) **What's next? Read and write.**

> fifteen   twenty   ~~eleven~~   twelve

1 one, three, five, seven, nine, ___*eleven*___
2 two, four, six, eight, ten, _____ , fourteen
3 three, six, nine, twelve, _____ , eighteen
4 five, ten, fifteen, _____

8 **Count and write. Then answer the questions.**

12					

1 How many socks are there?   *There are twelve socks.*
2 How many fish are there?   _____
3 How many cars are there?   _____
4 How many shoes are there?   _____
5 How many balls are there?   _____
6 How many books are there?   _____

9 🎧 4.11 Read and write the letter. Then listen and check.

a Let's tidy up! **b** Thanks, iPal! **c** It's your ring, Tina!

d Look at this big bookcase! **e** Oh no! Where's my ring?

f Now it's tidy.

1 e Is it in the art set?

2 There's my doll. We're in my bedroom!

3 Let's go in. Walk on me!

4 What a mess!

5 Let's put the toys in the cupboard.

6 What has iPal got?

Look, read and stick.

I am tidy.

11 **Trace the letters.**

Meerkats have got mouths. Newts have got noses.

12 **Listen and circle the pictures.**

m

n

How many are there?

1 Count and write the number.

1

 + = ☐

2

 + = ☐

3

 + = ☐

4

 + = ☐

Evaluation

1 **Order the letters and write the word.**

1 mlpa *lamp*

2 abetl _____

3 ccklo _____

4 hepno _____

5 mrrroi _____

6 fsao _____

2 **What's your favourite part? Use your stickers.**

story   song   video

3 **Puzzle** **What's different? Circle and write. Then go to page 93 and write the letters.**

___ ___ ___ ___ ___ ___ ___ ___
      3   6

Review Units 3 and 4

1 Look and write the word. Then draw Number 9.

```
                            9
                       1  c  l  o  c  k
              2           o     s
                       3        h     e
                 4  t           l
                 5     h        s
                    6           p
              7        i  r     o
                    8        r  s
```

9

2 Read and circle.

1 (There's) / There are a table in the kitchen.
2 What **is** / **are** you wearing?
3 How many bookcases **are** / **is** there?
4 This is a yellow **dress** / **jeans**.

3 Look, read and write the answers.

1

Is it ugly? ___No, it isn't.___

2

Are you wearing a jacket, Simon?

_____

3

What are you wearing, Grandma?

_____

4

How many socks are there in the wardrobe? _____

4 (4.17) Listen and tick ✓.

1

2

5 Meals

1 Find and circle. Look and write the word.

 1

_____rice_____

2

_____

3

_____

 4

_____

5

_____

6

_____

peascarrotscereal(rice)toastfish

2 Look, read and write *yes* or *no*.

1 There's meat on the table.
_____yes_____

2 There are peas on the table.

_____

3 There are potatoes on the table. _____

4 There are sausages on the table. _____

5 There's cereal on the table.

_____

3 🎧 5.05 ✂ Listen and stick.

| 1 | 2 | 3 |

| 4 | 5 |

4 (Think) Look and write the words.

~~toast~~ cereal peas rice meat
fish sausages potatoes carrots

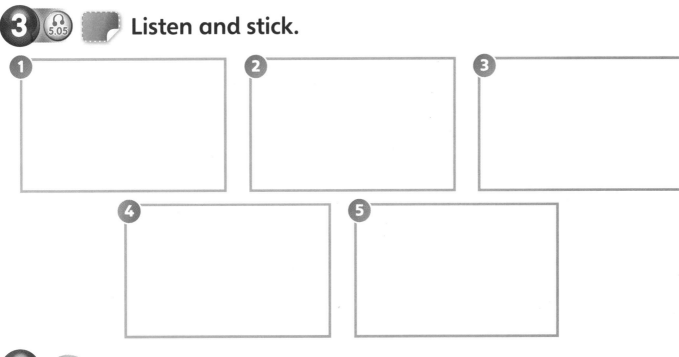

These foods are plants.	These foods aren't plants.
toast	

My picture dictionary Go to page 89: Tick the words you know and trace.

Vocabulary **49**

5 **5.08** **Listen and match. Draw a happy face or a sad face.**

6 **Look, read and circle the words.**

She **likes** / **doesn't like** fish.

He **likes** / **doesn't like** cereal.

She **likes** / **doesn't like** meat.

He **likes** / **doesn't like** peas.

Look, read and circle the words. Answer the questions.

Kim

Jim

1 Does Kim like (cereal) / sausages?
Yes, she does.

2 Does Kim like **toast** / **peas**?
No, she doesn't.

3 Does Kim like toast for breakfast?
_____ *Yes, she does.* _____

4 Does Kim like sausages?
_____

1 Does Jim like **carrots** / **potatoes**?
Yes, he does.

2 Does Jim like **steak** / **fish**?
No, he doesn't.

3 Does Jim like carrots for lunch?
_____

4 Does Jim like potatoes?
_____

  Draw and say. Then write and circle.

My mum likes meat and carrots for dinner. She doesn't like fish.

My _____ likes _____ and _____ for dinner. He / She doesn't like _____ .

9 Look and write the words. Then listen and check.

likes   fish   please   ~~lunch~~   peas   Cake

1

Look! Café Hawaii!

Café Hawaii

Let's go for _lunch_ !

2

Café Hawaii

Would you like _____ and potatoes?

Yes, please!

No, thank you!

3

What about carrots or _____, iPal?

No, thank you!

4

Oh dear! What would you like, iPal?

_____ ! I like chocolate cake.

5

More cake, _____ !

No, iPal. That's enough!

6

What's the matter?

He _____ chocolate cake – a lot!

10 **Look, read and stick.**

I eat healthy food.

11 **Trace the letters.**

A seal in the sun. A zebra in the zoo.

12 5.14 **Listen and circle s or z.**

1

(S) Z

2

S Z

3

S Z

4

S Z

What type of food is it?

1 Look and write the words in the table.

peas   sausages   rice   carrots

fish   cheese   milk   bread

fruit and vegetables	meat and fish	grains and cereals	dairy
peas			

Evaluation

1 **Read and write the word.**

1 T o a s t is bread.
2 C _ _ _ _ _ _ _ are orange. They come from plants.
3 F _ _ _ live in water. They can swim.
4 P _ _ _ are very small and green. They come from plants.
5 Chicken and sausages are m _ _ _ .
6 R _ _ _ is small and white. It comes from plants.

2 **What's your favourite part? Use your stickers.**

story   song   video

3 **Puzzle** **What's different? Circle and write.**
Then go to page 93 and write the letters.

___ ___ ___ ___
4   16

6 Activities

1 Think! Look, match and write.

 1
 2
 3
 4

a

ride a _____

b

play _____

c

fly a _____

d

take _photos_

2 Look and write the words.

play   take   ride   fly   play   rollerskate

 1

 2

 3

A: Let's play tennis. Can you _play_ tennis?
B: No, I can't, but I can _____ basketball.

A: Can you _____ a horse?
B: Yes, I can and I can _____ a kite, too.

A: I can rollerskate. Can you _____ ?
B: No, I can't, but I can _____ photos!

3 **Listen and stick.**

4 **Look and write the words.**

> ride a horse   ~~play basketball~~   play tennis
> rollerskate   take photos   play baseball

play basketball

My picture dictionary → Go to page 90: Tick the words you know and trace.

Vocabulary **57**

Look at the table. Circle the words and write.

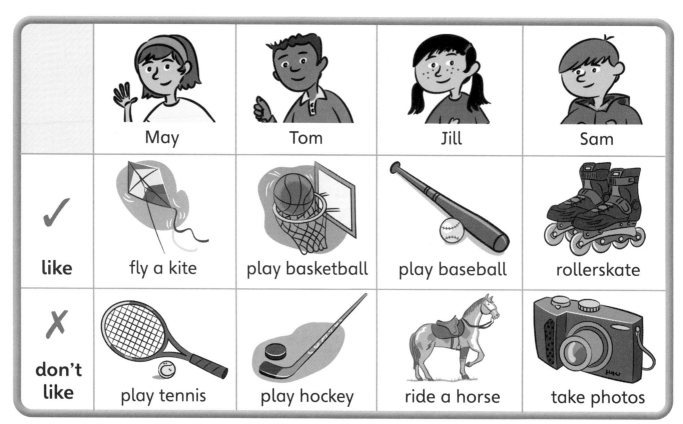

	May	Tom	Jill	Sam
✓ **like**	fly a kite	play basketball	play baseball	rollerskate
✗ **don't like**	play tennis	play hockey	ride a horse	take photos

1

I **like** /
~~**don't like**~~
playing tennis.

2

I **like** /
don't like
playing hockey.

3

I **like** /
don't like
riding a horse.

4

I **like** /
don't like
rollerskating.

5 May _____likes_____ flying a kite.

6 Tom _____ playing basketball.

7 Jill _____ playing baseball.

8 Sam _____ taking photos.

6 Look, read and circle the answers.

1

Do you like taking photos?

(Yes, I do.) / No, I don't.

2

Do you like playing tennis?

Yes, I do. / No, I don't.

3

Does he like playing baseball?
Yes, he does. / No, he doesn't.

4

Does she like flying a kite?
Yes, she does. / No, she doesn't.

7 (About Me) Complete the table. Ask and answer.

Do you like horse riding?   Yes, I do.

No, I don't.

Do you like …	riding a horse?	_____ ?	_____ ?
1 Me	yes / no	yes / no	yes / no
2 _____	yes / no	yes / no	yes / no
3 _____	yes / no	yes / no	yes / no

I like …

_____ likes …

Read and number. Then listen and check.

a

b

c

d

e

f

9 **Look, unscramble and stick.**

a   **b**

I (lypa) _____ nicely.

10 **Trace the letters.**

A camel with a camera. A kangaroo with a kite.

11 (6.14) **Listen and number the pictures.**

a

b

c

d

e 1

f

What equipment do we need?

1 Look and match the pictures.

2 Look at Activity 1 and write the words.

1 I play basketball with a ___basket___ and a ___ball___ .
2 I play tennis with a _____ and a _____ .
3 I play baseball with a _____ and a _____ .
4 I play hockey with a _____ and a _____ .

Evaluation

1 Think **Look and write the activity.**

1 r _ollerskate_

2 p_____ b_____

3 r_____ a
   h_____

4 p_____ t_____

5 p_____ h_____

6 p_____ b_____

2 What's your favourite part? Use your stickers.

story   song   video

3 Puzzle **What's different? Circle and write.
Then go to page 93 and write the letters.**

_ _ _ _ _ _ _ _ _ _ _ _ _ _
        15   5

63

Review Units 5 and 6

1 Write and draw.

a	b	c	d	e	f	g	h	i	k	l	o	p	r	s	t	u	y
1	2	3	4	5	6	7	8	9	10	11	12	13	14	15	16	17	18

1

p o t a t o e s
13 12 16 1 16 12 5 15

2

‾ ‾ ‾ ‾ ‾ ‾ ‾ ‾
6 11 18 1 10 9 16 5

3

‾ ‾ ‾ ‾ ‾ ‾ ‾ ‾
15 1 17 15 1 7 5 15

4

‾ ‾ ‾ ‾ ‾ ‾ ‾ ‾ ‾ ‾ ‾ ‾ ‾
13 11 1 18 2 1 15 10 5 16 2 1 11 11

5

‾ ‾ ‾ ‾ ‾ ‾
3 5 14 5 1 11

6

‾ ‾ ‾ ‾ ‾ ‾ ‾ ‾ ‾ ‾ ‾
14 12 11 11 5 14 15 10 1 16 5

2 Read and match.

1 He likes
2 She doesn't
3 Does he
4 I like playing
5 He doesn't like
6 Do you like

a hockey.
b beans.
c taking photos?
d toast.
e like playing tennis?
f like meat.

64

3 **Look, read and write the words.**

rollerskating   rice   ~~photos~~   fish   ~~do~~   doesn't   does   don't

1

Do you like taking _photos_ ?

Yes, I ___do___ .

2

Does she like _____ ?

Yes, she _____ .

3

Does he like _____ ?

No, he _____ .

4

Do you like _____ ?

No, I _____ .

4 🎧 6.17 **Listen and tick ✓.**

1

2
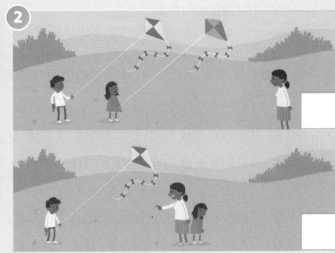

In town

1 **Look at the picture and write the letter.**

1 street __e__   2 café _____
3 school _____   4 bookshop _____
5 playground _____   6 supermarket _____

2 **Look at Activity 1 and write *yes* or *no*.**

1 There's a toy shop in the town.   __no__
2 There's a playground in the town.   _____
3 There's a cinema in the town.   _____
4 There's a café in the town.   _____
5 There's a clothes shop in the town.   _____
6 There's a school in the town.   _____

3 🎧 7.05 **Listen and stick.**

1.

2.

3.

4.

5.

4 Think **Look and write.**

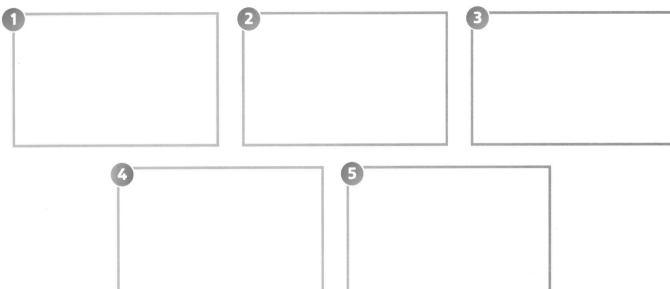

1.

toy shop

2.

3.

4.

My picture dictionary ➡ **Go to page 91: Tick the words you know and trace.**

Think **Look, read and match.**

1 next to

2 in front of

3 behind

4 between

6 **Look, read and circle the words.**

1 The school is **behind / next to** the playground.

2 The toy shop is **in front of / between** the bookshop and the clothes shop.

3 The tree is **next to / in front of** the cinema.

4 The supermarket is **behind / between** the park.

7 **About Me** **Draw and say. Then write.**

My school is next to the park.

My school is _____ _____ .

8 **Look, read and tick ✓.**

1 Is there a toy shop next to the school?

Yes, there is. ☐ No, there isn't. ✓

2 Is there a café in front of the supermarket?

Yes, there is. ☐ No, there isn't. ☐

3 Is there a toy shop between the book shop and the school?

Yes, there is. ☐ No, there isn't. ☐

4 Is there a playground behind the school?

Yes, there is. ☐ No, there isn't. ☐

9 **Complete the questions and the answers.**

1 _____Is there_____ a park next to the book shop?
No, _____there isn't_____ .

2 _____ a playground between the school and the supermarket?
No, _____ .

3 _____ a street in front of the café?
Yes, _____ .

4 _____ a park behind the supermarket?
Yes, _____ .

10 🎧 7.11 Read and write the letter. Then listen and check.

a No, iPal! Be careful!

b I like going to the cinema.

c Cinema tickets!

d Oh no! It's closed today!

e Look left and right.

f Where's the cinema?

1 C
They're from my cousin, Anna!

2 SUPERMARKET
It's next to the supermarket.

3 Let's go!
WAIT

4 It's safe now. Let's cross.

5 CLOSED
NOW SHOWING
The Queen
Come with me!

6 It's a film about robots!

11 Look, unscramble and stick.

I am (esfa) _____ .

12 Trace the letters.

A quick queen bee. An ox with an x-ray.

13 🎧 7.14 Listen and write *q* or *x*.

1

queen bee

2

6

si__

3

o__

4

__ueue

Where are the places?

1 Look, read and circle the word.

1 There's a (fire station) / **police station** in A3.

2 There's a **cinema** / **bookshop** in C3.

3 There's a **café** / **hospital** in B2.

4 There's a **sports centre** / **park** in D1.

2 Look at Activity 1 and answer the questions.

1 Where's the police station?   B1

2 Where's the bookshop?   _____

3 Where's the hospital?   _____

4 Where's the sports centre?   _____

Evaluation

1 **Look and write the word.**

1. supermarket
2. _____
3. _____
4. _____
5. _____
6. _____

2 **What's your favourite part? Use your stickers.**

story   song   video

3 **What's different? Circle and write.
Then go to page 93 and write the letters.**

| 9 | 13 |

8 On the farm

1 Look, read and circle the word.

1
(cow) / horse

2
sheep / goat

3
barn / field

4
horse / donkey

5
field / pond

6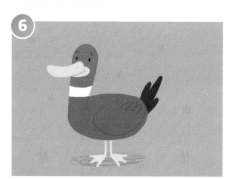
duck / donkey

2 Follow the animal words.

Start →

cow	goat	park	barn
field	duck	sheep	air
hospital	grains	donkey	school
dairy	pond	cat	horse

Well done!

3 🎧 8.05 **Listen and stick.**

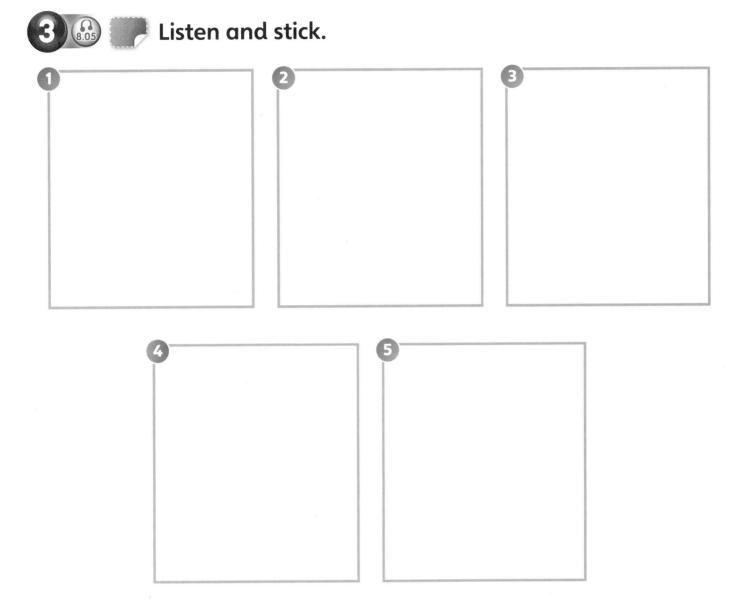

4 Think **Read and write the word.**

1 Milk comes from this animal. It isn't a goat. ___COW___
2 This animal can swim and fly. It likes water. _____
3 We can ride this animal. It's not a donkey. _____
4 Wool comes from this animal. _____
5 This is a house for cows and horses. _____
6 Fish and ducks swim in this. _____

My picture dictionary ➜ Go to page 92: Tick the words you know and trace.

5 Look, read and tick ✓.

1

The cow is eating. ✓

The cow is jumping. ☐

2

The horse is running. ☐

The horse is sleeping. ☐

3

The duck is flying. ☐

The duck is swimming. ☐

6 Look, read and answer the questions.

1

What's the donkey doing?

It's eating.

2

What's the duck doing?

_____

3

What's the goat doing?

_____

4

What's the sheep doing?

_____

7 (About Me) Draw your favourite farm animal. Then write.

This is a _____ .

It's _____ .

8 🎧 8.09 **Listen and tick ✓ or cross ✗.**

① 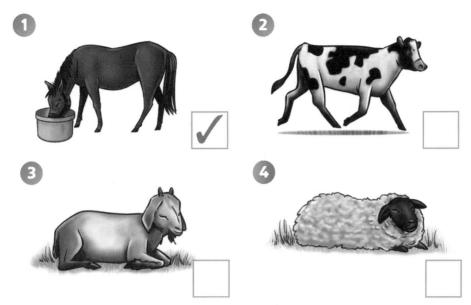 ✓

②

③

④

9 **Look, read and circle the word.**

①

Is the horse **eating** / (sleeping)?
No, it isn't.

②

Is the cow **running** / **sleeping**?
No, it isn't.

③

Is the goat **sleeping** / **eating**?
Yes, it is.

④

Is the duck **swimming** / **flying**?
Yes, it is.

⑤

Is the sheep **eating** / **running**?
No, it isn't.

⑥

Is the horse **sleeping** / **swimming**?
Yes, it is.

10 🎧 8.11 Look and write the words. Then listen and check.

party ~~iPal~~ dancing Goodbye flying Welcome

1

It's a message for ___iPal___ .

Let's find him!

2

Would you like to come to a _____?

Yes, please!

3

Hold on!

We're _____!

4

_____ to the party!

It's so nice to see you!

WELCOME HOME iPAL

5

What's Ben doing?

He's … _____!

6

_____, iPal!

Goodbye! Thanks for looking after me!

11 **Look, unscramble and stick.**

I love my (ehmo) _____ .

12 **Trace the letters.**

A wolf in the water.
A white whale with
a wheel.

13 🎧 8.14 **Listen and tick ✓ w or wh.**

1	w ✓	wh ☐	2	w ☐	wh ☐
3	w ☐	wh ☐	4	w ☐	wh ☐

What do farmers do?

1 Look and number.

2 Look at Activity 1 and write the letter.

1 A farmer turns the soil. `b`

2 A farmer plants the seeds.

3 A farmer waters plants.

4 A farmer harvests plants.

Evaluation

1 Write the words and find.

1. COW
2. _____
3. _____
4. _____
5. _____
6. _____

```
s h e e p a c n (c o w) o
g a d o n k e y m k l p
c b a r n o l p a t u e
f i e l d g h n a o q i
a f p o n d g r t e y a
```

2 What's your favourite part? Use your stickers.

story   song   video

3 Puzzle What's different? Circle and write. Then go to page 93 and write the letters.

____ ____ ____ ____
7   18

Review Units 7 and 8

1 Look and write the word. Then draw Number 11.

1. p o n d

2 Look, read and write the answers.

1

What's the goat doing?

_____It's jumping_____ .

2

Is there a park next to
the supermarket?

_____

3

Is the sheep running?

_____

4

What's the horse doing?

_____

3 🎧 8.17 Listen and tick ✓.

1

2

Hello again!

1 ✓ one

2 ☐ two

3 ☐ three

4 ☐ four

5 ☐ five

6 ☐ six

7 ☐ seven

8 ☐ eight

9 ☐ nine

10 ☐ ten

1 Transport

bus ✓

boat ☐

car ☐

helicopter ☐

lorry ☐

motorbike ☐

plane ☐

tractor ☐

train ☐

baby ✓

boy

cat

dog

fish

frog

girl

man

mouse

woman

3 Clothes

 ✓

dress

 ☐

jacket

 ☐

jeans

 ☐

shirt

 ☐

shoes

 ☐

skirt

 ☐

socks

 ☐

trousers

 ☐

T-shirt

(4) Rooms

bookcase ✓

clock

cupboard

lamp

mirror

phone

sofa

table

TV

wardrobe

5 Meals

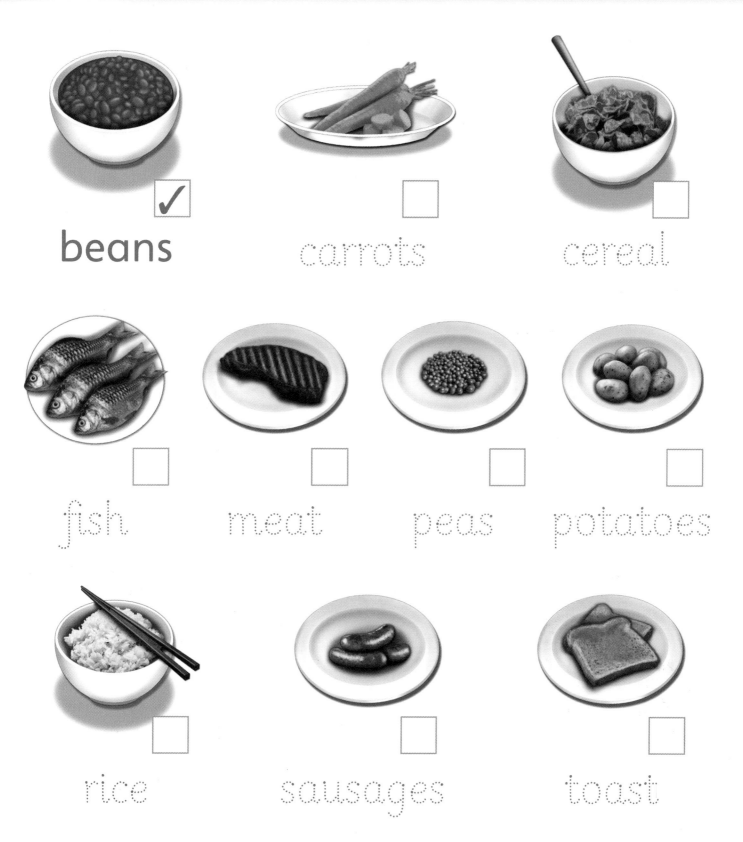

beans ✓

carrots

cereal

fish

meat

peas

potatoes

rice

sausages

toast

6 Activities

 ✓
fly a kite

 ☐
play baseball

 ☐
play basketball

 ☐
play hockey

 ☐
play tennis

 ☐
ride a horse

 ☐
rollerskate

 ☐
take photos

7 In town

book shop ✓

café

school

clothes shop

park

play-ground

cinema

street

supermarket

toy shop

8 On the farm

 ✓

barn

 ☐

cow

 ☐

donkey

 ☐

duck

 ☐

field

 ☐

goat

 ☐

horse

 ☐

pond

 ☐

sheep

My puzzle

1 Write the letters in the correct place.

1 2 3 4 5   6   7 8 9 10 11   12 13 14 15 16 17 18   !